Basic Survival Skills

30 Hacks and Tips to Get Prepped to Survive Anywhere In The World

Table of Contents

Introduction

Survival skills are important to learn for everyone. Its not necessary that if you are not survivor then you should not learn them. Survival skills can prove very helpful in any situation. The reason is that sometimes natural disasters can also put you in some such condition that you will have to leave your luxurious home. And certainly you have to find a place where you support yourself and your family members. So learning survival skills are crucial for everyone living any part of the world. But these skills are most important for the survivors when they often move alone in the wild or desert. These places are full of danger and one must acquire the basic survival skills before leaving cosy bed and delicious dinning.

Proper preparation and knowledge about different things is very necessary. Because in this way you would be able to face the threating situation. Those people who never learn survival skills are likely to lose in the wilderness and most of the times they become the food of the wild animals. So one must learn that how to rescue at the times when there is no other option left than to dying.

Surviving in abnormal situations is a thing that most of us never like. No one seems willing to leave comfortable life but sometimes nature forces us to do so. Contrary to it, survivors love to take challenges and put themselves in tough situations because they love to face threats and learn more. These things are adventurous for them and they spend several dollars for this purpose. They never go without survival skills at any such place which is full of extortions.

There are various TV programs as well that aim to provide you survival skills as well. These are also good source of learning but they show you limited skills that you can use only at some specific places or condition. But in this book you will find number of skills that you can use anywhere in the world. These skills are equally applicable in any situation where survival is necessary.

Chapter 1 – 10 Major Skills That Can Help You To Survive Anywhere In the World

In this chapter you will find 10 basic or major survival skills that are really very important to learn. No matter whether you are going for long hike, wild visit, desert travel or to face some natural disaster. These skills are primary survival skills and without acquiring them, you can't dream of returning to home safely. So, learn them earlier and follow the rule of self-reliance!

Survival Skill 01: Find Water

It is the basic necessity of life and you can't live without it. Food and shelter come later but the water is such a thing without that survival is impossible. This is the first, major and basic necessity of any individual. So what will you do if there is no water and the water you get is filthy and not drinkable? Certainly you won't like to drink the water that is full of germs and bacteria because in this way you will invite different diseases to come and catch you.

Keep your calm in any such situation and first of all try to find a place where there is water. There are several means of getting pure water. If you are knowledgeable person then you definitely know what actually those means are. But if you are unaware, its time to learn the skills to find water!

In the disastrous situation like floods, water often gets filthy. So you can directly gather rain water that is always pure and drinkable. Moreover, you can find some streams because these also contain drinkable water.

If you are in the wild and finding water is an issue then an easy thing that you can do is to follow the direction of birds. Because birds usually fly in that direction where there is water.

In case you aren't successful getting pure water, its time to purify it! You can sort out it by learning different that are discussed in the subsequent chapters.

Survival Skill 02: Find Food

Undoubtedly you can live without food for weeks but is it what you really want??? Even if you eat same type of food for several days, you get tired of it and face a problem known as food fatigue. So is it possible to imagine a life without food? You will definitely not die for weeks but you would be in worst possible situation. In the hot desert or dense wild you would not be able to walk for miles and ultimately death would be your destination.

Getting no food is another case but most of the times people are such ignorant that what to eat especially in the wild. There are certainly so many things in the wild that you can but when you are unaware and think that they might be poisoning then you avoid them.

When there is an alarming situation about some disaster its better to store food for it earlier. While in the desert you or wild you should acquire the knowledge about flora and fauna. So that you may learn that what are the edible foods and what type of herbs and plants are poisonous.

Often survivors eat certain insects as well. Because there is much fat in them and can help in surviving. So finding right type of food is an important survival skill that one must learn because it will help you to survive anywhere in the world.

Survival Skill 03: Build Shelter

When the other two basic needs are fulfilled, its time to build a shelter for you and your family. Building shelter requires some skills and you might be in need of a partner to help you for this. First find a place that is good enough where you can build a shelter. If there is a chance of heavy rain or flood then don't chose the ground or area that is near to river or sea. Choosing the right place for shelter is another skill. In the wild don't choose a place at the top or bottom rather somewhere in the middle. At the top your shelter will fell down due to winds.

Apart from this you can build a shelter with the help of tent, woods or leaves. Moreover some people sue space blanket. This blanket is not only helpful to build a reasonable shelter but also its very light weight and it can also be used to collect water. Survivors often build a shelter with some tree but you should learn that how to construct a safe one. Because in the wild different wild animals are also there so protection from them is also necessary.

Survival Skill 04: Build Fire

Without building fire its very difficult to sustain life. Its not your kitchen where you will use just a matches or lighter and start cooking food. Rather its an outdoor place where there is a need to acquire a skill to build fire by using woods and other things like that.

Fire severs different purpose for survival. On one side it keeps you warm while on the other side it is used to cook food and boil water. Another advantage is that – it can be used for signalling. Also get the knowledge about the kindling, logs, fibrous material and tinder because these are some of the things that help in building fire and can keep you warm at cold nights.

Survival Skill 05: Prepare Survival Kit

Prepper usually prepare a survival kit when they are likely to face some danger or threat. This survival kit or bug out bag is crucial to maintain earlier when there is some seasonal disaster such as flood. Most of the countries often face earthquakes and terrorist attacks very often so people living out there must plan to prepare a survival kit. This type of bug out bag/kit can help them to survive for at least 72 hours. No matter in what part of the world you are living, this little bag can help you to survive anywhere in the world.

Your bag must include such food that is low weight and full of calories. Some other things like torch, knife, map etc. should also be present in it. Survivors often put 30 different item in this bag for survival. According to the needs the item might differ but some basic things like plastic water bottles, lighter, snack bars, battery etc. remain the same.

If you have some toddler or babies at home then also put the things they would need. But remember, your bug out bag shouldn't be so heavy because you wouldn't be in a position to carry it and move.

Survival Skill 06: Purify Water

After finding water you are supposed to purify it but without acquiring different water purification skills you wouldn't be in a position to do this. So learn appropriately how to purify it. Without clean water there is no possibility of life. You would be live just for three days without water. So its very major survival technique that you should learn. There are several water purification methods such as heating, boiling, using chlorine tablets, iodine, chemicals, other drops, ultraviolet light, distillation and much more. Purified water will give you a new life and you would be able to move and continue your journey. This survival skill is essential as without it you are away from different diseases that are likely to catch you such as diarrhoea. Moreover, you also remain safe from other stomach diseases because the germs and bacteria that are the reasons to cause them exist no more.

Survival Skill 7: Navigation Method

When the threat is over you or when you are done with your visit to wild or desert, you like to navigate from such place. Sometimes it really becomes difficult to navigate when there is no communication and you are lost in dense wild. There are some skills that you can use to navigate. In addition they are likely to help you to survive. Those people who start visiting such strange place without proper planning and information, stuck there and never come back. So learn that how to navigate when the things are not in your favour.

There are several navigation skills and I consider them one of the major skills. Because without them you will never survive and return home safely. At that time you need help of someone, you wait and wish someone to come and rescue you. Its possible only at that time when you give them clue. There are certain other people who come for adventure. You can use mirror, dark clothes for flags, fire or whistle to let others know that you want help.

Most of the times survivals build fire and its smoke informs others that you need their help.

Survival Skill 08: First Aid

This is another important survival skill that can help you to survive anywhere in the world. Keep your first aid kit always ready and learn to use different things that are present inside. Such as learn to use different injections in case some wild animal bites you. Learn to know how to bandage in case of any injury. Hence, all little small things that can help you to survive are important to learn. Don't ever forget to put first aid kit in your bug out bag because it will save you and your family members as well.

Survival Skill 09: Protect Yourself

It's the need to protect yourself from different threats and dangers in the wild. Because you don't want to become the food of wild animals. Your protection is your utmost priority. So learn that what to do when a wild animal is in from of you. Snakes are very common in the wild. On one side they can bite you while on the other hand you can use their meat to cook delicious food. But all this needs skills. Without the survival skills you wouldn't be in a position to make good out of bad things.

Not only in the wild but also in different disaster situations or during hike you can face security issues. The basic survival protection skills will help you to survive anywhere in the world.

Survival Skill 10: Use Survival Knife

It is also one of the major survival skills. Without survival knife your bug out bag is incomplete. A survival knife can perform several purposes such as it can use to cut rope, build fire, build shelter, cut food, discourage wild animals and so on. It must be very sharp and always ready. It can also be a pocket knife as well. But among other survival tools, its considered best. The reason is that it's not heavy and you can carry it anywhere with bit ease and comfort.

Hence, the above mentioned skills are considered as major skills because these are integral part of any survival condition. Without acquiring these skills you can't prevent yourself from the dangers ahead. These skills are applied worldwide and help you to survive anywhere in the world. To learn them is crucial for everyone because you never know when a disaster strikes with you. Learn to live a rule of self-reliance by learning these major survival skills.

Chapter 2 – 10 Minor Skills That Can Help You To Survive Anywhere In The World

The skilled discussed in this chapter are somewhat major and minor. In other words these skills are closely related to major skills. These skills also support the major skills in many ways. We can also term them as sub skills as well. The major skills are crucial but when you will learn these skills, you will tackle the things in more appropriate way. Let's discuss them in brief:

Survival Skill 11: Make Adequate Search

Expert survivors and adventurists suggest that make a proper research before leaving your home. The search is important in so many ways and it has several advantages as well. Prior search enables you to think wisely and in this way you properly plan your journey. Whenever you decide to go somewhere make sure that you have the knowledge about that region. During the disaster you are likely to leave your home in hurry so you don't find any time to make search. But still you can acquire general information about the location where you aim to depart. This type of information can be obtained by talking to some people in a good manner or some helping/rescue teams. Moreover, on radio usually different programs start with the aim to help you move successfully. So keep a small radio with you always so that you may be aware of different threats through news.

Apart from this, search for survivalist helps them to ascertain the threat ahead. When they make a proper search they know that how they can navigate from such place when they are stuck. Besides they also come across the fact that what type of wild animals are there. In this way they can make necessary adjustments to protect themselves.

Survival Skill 12: Learn to Study Map

Its an important survival tip as it assist to move in a right direction. Bug out bag also contain a map as well. But if you have a map and don't know how to read it then its useless to keep it. Map will also guide and assist you about the location where you would be able to get water in case of emergency. It will also show you the dense areas where there is threat and you shouldn't move in that direction.

Survival Skill 13: Learn to Use Compass

Keep a compass in your BoB. This is definitely going to help you when you will find no way to go. In the wild or somewhere else when you are lost, this compass will show you the directions. So you can choose the one that can take you out from that particular location. Basically its needles show the directions. Therefore when you start your journey, check the direction first, later on when you stuck, you can easily find that from where you started.

Survival Skill 14: Use Mind

Your mind is the most important thing that you have and there is no alternative of it. One of the survival skills is learn to use your mind. If you get panic in difficult situation then you will not be in a position to get back home. This survival skills can also be considered as a major skill because without it you can't move on. Whenever you face any stressful situation, learn to overcome this. Never let the things grab you. You can find your way by staying positive and optimistic. Survivalists suggest you a simple tip for it and that is STOP. It means that 'Sit down', after that 'Think', then 'Observe' and finally 'Prepare' yourself to move on!

Survival Skill 15: Make Rope

Its another surviving skill that can help you for building shelter, lifting weights and so many other things. Different types of knots serves different purposes. Tie rope with one tree and cross a river, pond or any other such place. In any tough situation you can get maximum out of it. Learn to make pulleys and different knots to survive anywhere in the world.

Survival Skill 16: Earth Oven

Earth oven severs many purposes and it can be made very easily. By simply using stones and mud, you can make earth oven. It aids to cook food easily. Moreover you can use it to boil or heat water. It can help to keep you warm in days and at nights. You can cook on it without having any special utensil or pot. Survivalists often cook the fish directly on the hot stones as well. But to do such unique things, some skills are required that you can get easily by learning.

Survival Skill 17: Cooking Skills

Nobody wants to die with huger. We make efforts for survival. Whether it's a disaster or some other such situation, sometimes you need to cook food. And you can do it only in that case when you have skills to cook. Here cooking food doesn't mean to make a delicious meal. Rather it refers to cook food when there is no stove, fire, veggies or meat. In such situation what will you do? Definitely you will find food by hunting or fishing or anything else, then building earth oven and fire and so on. Sometimes you often don't have any pots as well. Then learn how to cook without pots as well.

Survival Skill 18: Learn how to trap

This survival skill is of utmost importance as you learn that how to trap different animals, hunt them and use them for making delicious food. Whether you are in a desert or wild, this skill will guarantee you that you will never die with hunger.

Survival Skill 19: Get Info. About Flora

It's the knowledge about plants of that particular habitat. Those people who are equipped with the knowledge of flora of different regions, they find a lot of plants to it and use as medicines. As we know that some plants especially more than few herbs can be used to cure different diseases. Those people who have a vast knowledge about flora are likely to face less survival problems. Some plants and herbs are poisonous, so they know the difference very well. In this way they know that what to eat and what to avoid. On the contrary, those people who have least or almost no knowledge about flora are likely to face several issues. The past data shows that there are number of people who die just because of the reason that they use wrong plants to survive especially in the wild.

Survival Skill 20: Get Info. About Fauna

After flora you are required to get proper knowledge of fauna of that particular habitat. It relates to knowledge about different animals of different regions. Like flora you will also learn that what type of animals can be hunt and what type of animals are likely to exist in some specific region. Some animals can also be used for ride. So it's up to you that how you get maximum out of them

The survival skills mentioned in the above lines prove very vital to survive in rough and tough conditions. Some basic information about fauna and flora, using mind, making rope and building oven etc. can take you away from disastrous and dangerous situation.

Chapter 3 – 10 Other Skills That Can Help You To Survive Anywhere In The World

Here in this chapter you will learn some other skills that can help you to survive anywhere in the world. The skills discussed in the previous two chapters are more important compared to these ones. But the importance of these skills can't be overwhelmed. Let's discuss these survival skills in brief:

Survival Skill 21: Knowledge about Injections

Sometimes it becomes important to get the information about the injections. Those people who have faced different disaster or worst situations can tell you better the importance of acquiring this skills. At the time of disasters many diseases spread. Apart from this survivalists also face some unbearable situations. In the wild snake bites are common so you must have injections that can help to at that time. Otherwise their poison will take you to the verge of death. There are some other vaccines that you can use as well when some diseases spread due to disasters. The knowledge about these basic things can help you to survive anywhere in the world.

Survival Skill 22: Pick Up Right Blanket

In case of any emergency when you are supposed to leave your home instantly, don't forget to take with you a blanket. Taking blanket doesn't mean that use some very cosy blanket. Rather it means to carry some survival blanket. Survival blankets are usually different and light weight. Moreover, these can be used for several purpose. They not only prevent you from harsh weather but also helps you to collect water and build shelter. So picking up the right blanket is also a skill that people often don't have. For survival purpose space blanket is considered better. Pick up this one with right size, too small often leads to some problems while too long is difficult to manage.

Survival Skill 23: Use Different Gadgets for Communication

Communication is very important in case of any emergency. Especially at that time when you are away from your family members and stuck somewhere in the wild. Not only in the wild but anywhere in the world, you should have mobile phone or portable CB radio. If there is a signal issue, you can use satellite communication devices as well. These devices are somewhat expensive but are vital to save you. So learn the skills to use latest gadgets for survival purpose.

Survival Skill 24: Hunting

You aren't allowed everywhere to hunt but in the wild or desert you can use this skill to get some food.

Survival Skill 25: Fishing

Fish are full of proteins so you can eat them when there you are hungry. Keep some necessary equipment with you that will help you to catch fish. Moreover you can easily cook it. It takes few minutes to cook and its really delicious. Fishing skill is very important to acquire so that you may survive when you are hungry.

Survival Skill 26: Make Sundial

Learning about how to make a sundial is important. If you have lost your watch it will help you to know the exact time of the day. This is easy to make and by following less than few steps you can make sundial. Time is an important element because due to it you would be able to find a shelter in the evening.

Survival Skill 27: Make Swedish Candle

In the night there is a need of light but all the time you can't have a bulb or torch. So learn a skill to make beautiful Swedish candles with less efforts and time. These candles are used not only for lighting purpose but you can use them to cook delicious food. Use your pocket knife or some other sharp tool to cut the log and make these candles. Place these candles at such place where there is no danger (means where there is no grass that is likely to catch fire).

Survival Skill 28: Predict Weather

Another skill that you can acquire is to predict weather. First of all don't choose any such place to where the weather is extremely harsh. Too cold and too hot places are often exposed to more threats. Moreover, make sure that there is no rain and if there is a chance then stop travelling/walking and build a shelter to protect yourself. When there is a danger birds and animals often make noise or there are dense clouds. So learn to predict weather through several ways.

Survival Skill 29: Site Selection

Choosing a right site for camping is crucial because it protects you and helps you in survival. As discussed in the first chapter of this book that never build shelter on the very top of the mountain or near to sea. Because these places bring more threats. Your purpose is survival and by picking up the right place for camping can save you and your family members.

Survival Skill 30: Learn Ways to Keep Food Cold

Either it's a disaster or you are in a desert or wild, there is a need to eat some food that has some nutritional value as well. You can't survive long by just eating same thing for several days. Food fatigue and other some psychological issues will start disturbing you. On the other hand the food that is full of proteins, carbs and other essential nutrients is likely to spoil very soon such as fist, meat etc. So there is a need to learn the skills that help you to keep the food cold for days. Use large ice cubes in the coolers and put such food in them so that you may use them longer. Moreover, you can also keep such food near river or snow but its also open to threats such as wild animals can eat it. Therefore, there is a need to eat healthy food while preventing it from dangers.

The above mentioned survival skills will definitely help you to survive anywhere in the world. So learn them and make survival easy for yourself and your family.

Conclusion

This book defined all the skills that can help an individual to survive anywhere in the world. No matter you have decided to go for long hike, to face threats or to strike with some disaster. These skills are likely to help you face every challenge at every place.

In all the chapters all those skills were discussed that can prove vital and do miracles. Those people who don't want to depend on others, no matter how tough the conditions are, they will learn a lot out of these skills. These skills can make an individual an independent person and he can live his life while facing threats happily.

So its important to take a decision now about learning these skills. On one hand such skills will save you from drastic situation while on the other hand you will not look for anyone's help. What often happen is that people start looking at others for help when the conditions are tough. But a person equipped with such skills will make a difference and help others as well.

Some basic skills like finding water, shelter, food, fire, stove etc. are important to acquire by an individual. Always prepare yourself for uncertain situations because disaster never inform anyone earlier. Learn the skills so that you may succeed in your life when others are wandering here and there. Moreover, inform your loved ones before leaving your home for wild journey and later on keep in touch with them. In case you are lost, at least they would be able to come and locate you. Because if you will not make best use of your skills, you are likely to face more threats. But again the importance of these skills can't be overwhelmed.

So experts and survivalist suggest you that learn and spread these skills and would be able to survive anywhere in the world.

FREE Bonus Reminder

PreppersLiving.com

If you have not grabbed it yet, please go ahead and download your special bonus report *"DIY Projects. 13 Useful & Easy To Make DIY Projects To Save Money & Improve Your Home!"*

Simply Click the Button Below

OR **Go to This Page**

http://preppersliving.com/free

BONUS #2: More Free Books

Do you want to receive more Free Books?

We have a mailing list where we send out our new Books when they go free on Kindle. Click on the link below to sign up for Free Book Promotions.

=> Sign Up for Free Book Promotions <=

OR Go to this URL

http://zbit.ly/1WBb1Ek

Made in United States
North Haven, CT
07 September 2022